first performance: Beth Pearson, September 24, 1994 at the Performing Arts Center, SUNY Purchase, NY

SUITE FOR SOLO CELLO

I. Preludio

duration: ca. 8 minutes

Andante, rubato

II. Fuga - Burletta

Allegro moderato

III. Sarabanda

Lento molto

IV. Giga

Prestissimo

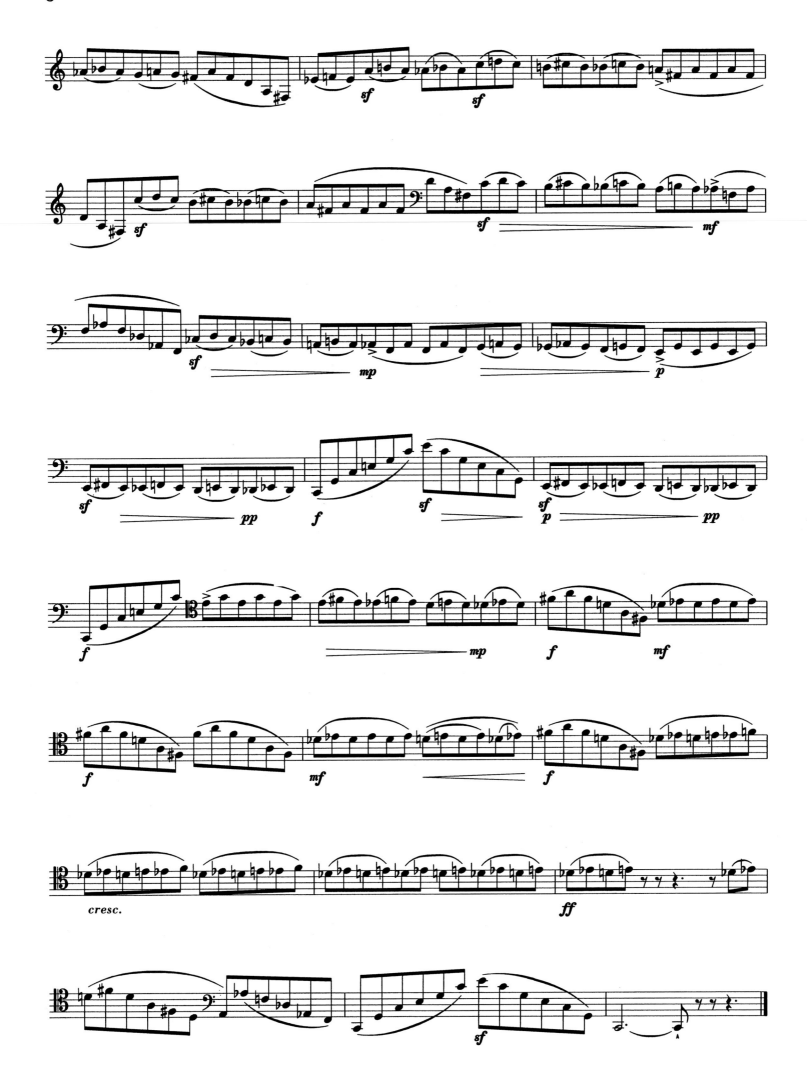